Herb Gardening

Illustrations by Carol Daniel
Written by Karen Kenny

TOP THAT!™

Copyright © 2005 Top That! Publishing Inc,
25031 W. Avenue Stanford,
Suite #60, Valencia, CA 91355
All rights reserved
www.topthatpublishing.com

Contents

History of Herbs

Herbs have been put to a wide variety of uses throughout the ages. They have been used as medicines, to enhance the flavor of foods, as perfumes, insecticides, dyes, and of course, to ward off evil spirits, and sometimes even to evoke them.

One of the earliest known "herbalists" was the great Chinese emperor Shen Nung (*c.*3000BC) who was known as "The Divine Healer".

Written evidence, in the form of medical texts on papyri, has also revealed that herbs were used in ancient Egypt. Probably the most well known of these is the Ebers papyrus which dates back to at least 1800BC.

In Greece the herbalist Asclepius, who later became the Greek god of medicine and healing, practiced sometime after 1250BC. Aided by his daughters Hygeia and Panace, their combined deeds later gave rise to a host of legends.

In his work *De Materia Medica*, Diascorides, a Greek army doctor from the 1st century, described over 500 plants and 1,000 medications. Diascorides' work remained the primary reference for the next 150 years. At the same time Pliny, a Roman physician, also wrote a work on plants and their medicinal uses. In it he theorized that the shape and color of the plants indicated its use in medicine, which later became known as the doctrine of signatures. During the Dark Ages herbalism was kept alive in the monasteries where herb gardens were tended, texts copied and herbal healing put into practice. Outside of religious orders "wise women" also gathered roots and herbs from the wayside and performed their "arts".

The earliest British herbalist was the Saxon monk Bald, who relied on both

ritual and magic and produced a work based on local plants called the *Leech Book of Bald* (*c*.950AD).

Probably the best-known herbalist of "modern times" is Nicholas Culpeper (1616–1654) who practiced in London's East End. Culpeper subscribed both to the theory of astrological botany (the planetary rulership of plants determining their medicinal use), as well as to the doctrine of signatures. Culpeper's theories remained the most comprehensive study of herbs until 1931 when Mrs M Grieves published *A Modern Herbal* which recorded both the usage and history of herbs.

Herbs in Medicine

Wise women, root gatherers, shamans, and medicine men have known the medicinal properties of many common plants for centuries.

The practical uses of herbs were discovered by trial and error. It was common practice to observe a plant, noting where it grew, its shape, and color. Then the herb would be crushed to release its essential oils and perfume before finally being tasted.

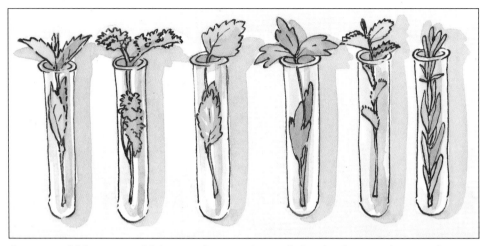

Some would have tasted bitter and unpalatable, others pleasant, while some would seem to cure ailments and give extra vitality, whereas many would have proved fatal!

The herbs used by these ancient people over the centuries have led to the modern array of medicines available over the counter and to physicians. Since these early trials, we have learned that herbs contain complex chemical structures. Their medicinal effects are due to the active principles or secondary plant products that they make, such as the alkaloids, glycosides, mucilage, bitters, essential oils etc.

Herbalists tend to use the whole herb, or the part of the herb with the medicinal effect, in the belief that the fresh or dried plant may contain other

substances which may have a balancing effect. This is apposed to the distillation of the active principles, which orthodox medicine uses.

A single herb used to treat a symptom is called a "simple". Combinations of herbs are also used now as the understanding of the bodily systems has evolved. The holistic approach takes into account lifestyle, diet, temperament and external influences and aims to recreate the balance of a healthy body, helping the body to heal itself.

Herbs are used in many ways and can be ingested or applied to the body directly. They can be taken raw, as decoctions (boiled), infusions, teas, tisanes, syrups, and herbal pills. They can also be made into tinctures (dissolved in alcohol), or essences (pressed and added to alcohol), essential oils, ointments, compresses, or poultices.

Herbs as Flavorings

During the Middle Ages methods of preserving food were very basic so herbs and spices were widely used, both to improve the flavor of bland food and to disguise the taste of rancid food!

Culinary herbs in the sixteenth century included sorrel, onions, and parsnips, which were classified as "pot herbs". The leaves and roots were both used and were either roasted or boiled and eventually became known as "vegetables".

Basil, sweet cecily, savory and so on were known as "sweet herbs" and were used solely for enhancing the flavor of a particular dish.

It is these sweet herbs which we tend to think of as the culinary herbs. Using them can reduce the need for salt in savory dishes, and sugar in sweet dishes.

Maybe the best-known combination of savory herbs, used for many years to flavor soups, stocks, stews, and casseroles, is the "bouquet garni" or "faggot of herbs". The three main ingredients are: a dried bay leaf, a few sprigs of fresh parsley, and a sprig of thyme tied together by the stems, so that they may be lifted from the stock or soup before serving.

Parsley

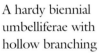

A hardy biennial umbelliferae with hollow branching stems with mid-green leaves densely curled. Green-yellow flowers on 23 in. (60 cm) stems in the second summer. Sow seeds in drills during February to June and lightly cover with soil. Best grown in well-drained, fertile soil, enriched with compost in a sheltered position with a southerly aspect.

In September sow more under glass for the winter supply and cut established plants back, covering with cloches for a continued supply of fresh leaves.

Properties: Rich in vitamins A and C with a distinctive, mildly spicy, flavor.

Culinary uses: To flavor sauces and stuffing, use in bouquets garnis and as a garnish for savory dishes.

Herbs as Teas & Tisanes

The discovery of tea is attributed to Emperor Shen Nung who was purportedly boiling water to purify it before drinking when a few leaves from an overhanging bush floated down into the water. He drank the resultant brew and found it quite efficacious and hence discovered a new beverage. *Camellia Sinensis*, or the tea plant, is now the most widely drunk herbal tea.

Herbal teas, as we think of them, are actually refreshing tisanes which are an integral part of the herbalist's medicine chest. They have been used to soothe, alleviate depression, invigorate, induce sleep, aid digestion, and even in childbirth.

Teas and tisanes are differentiated by their methods of production. Teas are made from herbs that have been harvested, dried or otherwise processed, such as smoked. Tisanes are made by the infusion of fresh herbs, or herbs that have been simply air-dried.

The usual method for making a herbal tisane is quite simple. It is best to use a glass or china pot, never a metal one. Pick three to six teaspoons of fresh herbs, according to taste, bruise them and pour over half a pint of boiling water. Cover for up to ten minutes and serve using honey as a sweetener if desired. You can substitute one teaspoon of the dried herb, when fresh herbs are not available.

Bergamot

A herbaceous perennial with hairy stems, rough oval, deep green serrated leaves and dense red whorled flowers from June to September.

Plant in moist soil in sun or partial shade during either October, March, or April. Alternatively grow from seed, in a cold frame in March, grow on and plant in flowering positions in October. Cut stems down in the fall and divide after three years, replanting outer new suckers.

The leaves are used to make Oswego tea (the name derives from the old American Indian tribe "Otsego" who lived in the area now known as New York, that once had an abundant supply of bergamot). It has a pleasing perfume reminiscent of the bergamot orange, which provides the oil that is used in Earl Grey tea.

Propagation by Seeds

Many of the common herbs that have become almost native plants over the centuries can easily be grown from seed without much trouble. The important thing is to prepare the soil in the previous season.

Most herbs are not too particular and will be quite happy in a well-drained, suitable soil. It is important that the seed bed is free of stones, holes, and cracks which fine seeds may disappear down. Make sure you till the soil to a nice friable, fine tilth within a flat bed and, when sowing seeds, cover with soil as indicated on the packet. Gently firm with the back of the rake; this makes sure the seeds are in intimate contact with the soil to assist water absorption and give them stability when they have rooted. It will also reduce surface evaporation.

Usually around April is the best time to sow but observe other growth in plants for a better indication. When weeds begin to emerge then you know the conditions are conducive for germination. Choose a dry day when the soil is easily worked and start to sow. However, if the soil is too dry then water the drills before sowing to give seeds a good start.

Sowing in Trays

Some exotic herbs may have difficulty
in the open ground and are best sown
in trays and potted before planting in
their permanent positions.

The timing of sowing seeds in trays is
equally important, especially if you do
not have a heated greenhouse or a cold
frame. The amount of light is crucial to
the steady growth and health of the
seedlings. Low light levels will give
spindly seedlings which are less likely
to make healthy plants later.

The compost you use is also very important. Do not be tempted to use an all-purpose compost; they may give reasonable results, but considering the small amount you need for germinating seeds it is best to buy a good quality compost specifically for seeds.

The use of seed trays for the initial germination of seeds is not always necessary. It is possible to sow in circular pots, which you will find supplied in this pack.

Crock your pots to ensure free drainage and fill with proprietary, soil-based seed compost to within an inch (2 cm) of the top. Firm well with a block made to fit the pot, and prevent the seeds from washing into the corners by making sure the surface is even, with no dips.

Water from above to settle the compost and ensure no tell-tale dips. Sow seeds lightly on the surface and cover with fine-sifted compost or vermiculite. As most seeds need darkness to germinate, cover them with newspaper. You will also find that bottom heat is beneficial but not essential.

Inspect the seedlings every day and as soon as the first shoots emerge, remove the newspaper, as light is essential for the seed to grow.

When growing in a window, make a light box. Start by covering the inside surfaces of a box with foil. Stand the box on its side with the tray slotted in so that the light is reflected around the plant effectively. This helps to avoid leggy, leaning seedlings. Remember to turn the pots daily.

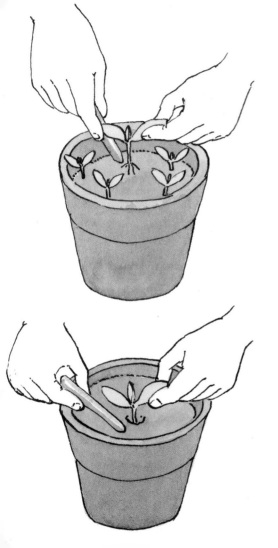

Pricking Out

As soon as seedlings have developed the first pair of true leaves it is time to prick out into pots or trays. Fill pots or trays with good-quality compost (soil-less composts will be fine for the faster-growing herbs) to the same levels as before and make a hole with a pen or dibber. Carefully hold the plant by its seed leaf and gently prize from the pot, trying not to damage the roots.

Pop into the ready-made hole and gently firm around the plant with the dibber, making sure it is in contact with the soil and has no air spaces around it. Place seedlings slightly lower in the compost than they were before.

Damping Off

Damping off refers to sudden plant death in the seedling stage due to an attack of fungi. These fungi are soil-borne and are stimulated by nutrients released during germination. However, seedlings may be injured, or killed, by other things —toxic materials in the soil, excess or deficient soil moisture, temperature extremes, and toxic gases in the air.

There is a preventative measure you can take to ward against damping off. Make a solution by pouring one pint of boiling water over 2 oz (57 g) of chamomile flowers, leaving to cool and strain. Dip seeds in and allow to dry before sowing. If the seeds are very small, sow them, then spray with the solution and allow to dry before covering.

Hardening Off

Before planting, your herbs need to be hardened off. Without this process all your previous efforts could be wasted, and it is important to be patient if you want good results. As the temperature warms up and the plants grow you need to acclimatise them gradually to life outside.

Start by placing the plants in a cold frame and slowly increase ventilation by raising the top slightly more with each

fine day and closing at night until it is removed during the day.

Then follow this process again at night. After a few weeks they should be ready for planting in their permanent positions.

If you do not have a cold frame then place plants outside in a sheltered place during the day and bring them in at night until you deem it safe to leave them out all night.

Taking Cuttings

Vegetative Propagation
Propagation from seed can produce variable plants while vegetative propagation ensures the characteristics of the parent plant remain.

Adequate light, warmth, moisture, and food reserves are essential for any cutting to form roots. The compost should be free-draining, moisture-retentive, and sterile.

Step 1   Step 2

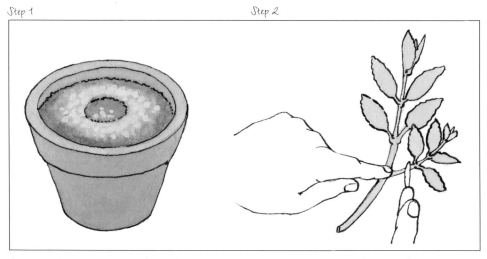

Step 1   Prepare a pot with seed compost. Top it up with a layer of sand, so that a few grains trickle down into the dibber holes, giving the rooting process a head start.

French tarragon can only be propagated by cuttings. Sage, thyme, lemon verbena, rosemary, lavender, and shrub herbs are also best propagated by cuttings.

Step 2   Cuttings taken in the growing season between late spring and early summer will root quickly. Choose a healthy young shoot with no disease or pest damage and sever just below a node (where the leaf joins the stem).

Place in a blown-up plastic bag to maintain humidity and to stop the cutting from drying out in transit. Remove the lower leaves and plant in

Step 3

Step 4

pots of previously watered and drained compost, in holes made by a dibber. Firm around the cutting to ensure contact with the soil.

Steps 3 & 4   Give the filled pots a final mist of water to settle the soil and refresh the leaves. Cover with a cloche made from a plastic bottle and place out of direct sunlight. When new growth starts to appear, gradually make

a few holes, each day, in the cloche until it can be removed completely. Continue to grow on in the pot.

Whilst you may grow several cuttings in a tray, you can also pot them individually. This can help them establish more quickly and root disturbance will be minimal when planting out.

Layering

Should you be nervous about your cuttings being successful then apply the extra-cautious technique of layering a few branches.

In spring, take one of the older branches close to the ground and peg it down firmly (use a wire pin at each end and a stone placed on top). Remember to remove any foliage coming into contact with the soil. Water regularly and, when roots have formed, sever from the old plant.

Division & Root Propagation

Some plants, such as St John's wort, form dense root clumps. These can simply be divided by separating the roots with two garden forks back to back. Make sure to re-plant immediately and water well.

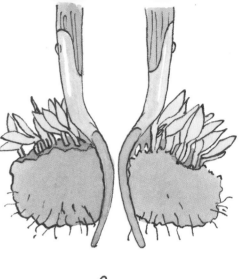

Herbs with creeping root systems (mints, bergamot etc.), are easily propagated. Simply cut a section from one of the horizontal roots coming from the main stem in spring and re-plant immediately.

With fleshy rooted herbs, like horseradish and Russian comfrey, carefully uproot the plants and with a sharp, sterile knife just cut the root offsets (root section with growing tip) and re-plant straight away.

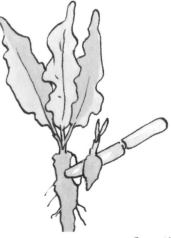

Herbs in Containers

Plants in containers enable everyone to enjoy the pleasures of herbs. They will supply you with your favorite herbs and can host a variety of combinations, whether you have room for just one container or several.

With provisions for drainage taken into account almost anything can be used when planting herbs, from an old zinc bathtub or pail, to terracotta pots (lined with plastic to reduce drying out), ceramic pots, wooden half-barrels, hanging baskets, to an old bicycle basket!

Whichever container you opt for ensure there are sufficient holes and then place a good layer of crocks, stones, gravel, or polystyrene in the bottom.

If your pot is large then plant up in its final position or use a stand on castors. Most herbs require a free-draining compost; however, for hanging baskets this can be too heavy so a proprietary soil-less compost will be fine.

Large, deep pots are best for containing large shrubby herbs like rosemary or bay, underplanted with a herbaceous mix.

Medium-sized pots suit a mixture of a single small, shrubby plant (lavender, hyssop, curry plant) together with thyme and marjoram trailing over the side. In a pot only a foot (thirty cm) in diameter you can plant three small plants, but remember to mix plants that have similar requirements.

An effective idea is to stack two or three different-sized pots on top of each other. Take the largest pot and fill with compost, then stack the second largest on top of that and fill with soil. Finally, place the smallest pot on top and fill with soil. Plant around the edge of the bottom pot with trailing herbs or tumbling tomatoes. Feathery herbs like dill will look good in the second pot. Choose something dramatic for the top pot—bergamot is a good choice.

Maintenance

Herbs in gardens do not normally need feeding. However, in containers they will soon use up the limited supply of nutrients and will need supplementing. A weekly feed of diluted seaweed feed should be adequate. Water more frequently according to the weather. In summer water daily and if a hot, dry spell persists, twice daily. Soak the compost until water comes out of the bottom. You can also mulch the top with gravel to conserve moisture and prevent weeds. During winter a container is susceptible to frosts, so for vulnerable pots, wrap in bubble wrap and group pots together, if possible on gravel to improve drainage.

Planting a Parsley Pot

Parsley is in demand all year for bouquets garnis, salads, as a garnish, tisanes, and for keeping the breath fresh. Plant up a parsley pot annually to keep a steady supply of good leaves throughout the year. You may find a strawberry pot is more suitable and accommodating than an average parsley pot, as it has a greater number of side holes.

Step 1

First place a roll of wire netting in the center of the pot and fill with stones, broken crocks, or rubble. Add a layer of crocks on the bottom. This is essential to make sure the water reaches all parts of the pot and drains well.

Step 2

Using good quality compost, start to

Step 1   Step 2   Step 3

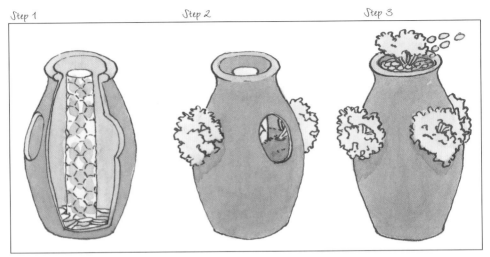

fill the pot, inserting plants in the holes as you fill. Ensure the plants are firmed in.

Step 3

Continue to fill until the final plants are placed in the top of the container around the roll of wire. Top off with a mulch of gravel to retain moisture.

Use a few leaves from each plant and your parsley pot will always look good

and balanced. Pinch off flower stems as they appear. Keep well watered, especially during hot weather.

Bring inside as the frosts start, preferably into a conservatory or greenhouse to give sufficient light for continued growth. Stand in a large saucer filled with gravel to allow good drainage and humidity around indoor plants.

Planting a Bay Tree

Bay leaves are an essential ingredient of bouquets garnis and can be used to flavor tomato-based sauces, soups, casseroles and so on. The leaves are often dried as this intensifies the aromatic properties of the herb.

While young, the trees can be susceptible to frosts and are frequently grown in pots that can be moved into shelter during the winter months.

Bays are slow-growing and hence a fully-grown one is expensive. However, they can be both ornamental and useful features in the garden, especially when pruned into the standard lollipop bays seen gracing decked areas.

Step 1   Step 2   Step 3

Step 1
Place broken crocks in the base to ensure good drainage; if training a standard place a stake in the pot.

Step 2
Then partially fill with compost. Remove the young bay from the old pot and place into a new container. Fill to previous planting depth, leaving a watering space of 2 in. (5 cm) from the rim.

Step 3
Water and top with a layer of gravel as mulch and to stop weed growth.

To develop a standard lollipop shape, trim off the lower branches, flush with the main stem, and support by loose ties to the stake. When it reaches the desired height start pinching out the tips to make the head branch out and form a ball. Remove any buds and branches that appear on the main stem.

Window Boxes

If you don't have room for a herb garden, or simply don't have a garden, then a box or trough of herbs sitting on the window ledge throughout the year is an attractive alternative.

Rather than planting up a trough it can be much better to fill it with individual pots of herbs. Supermarkets sell herbs in pots now and these are a useful source for the window ledge. Take them home and re-pot, pinch and give them a chance to recover.

Small pots of perennials and annuals can be changed at regular intervals to suit the latest culinary fashion. Lemon grass teamed with coriander and Thai basil will create a taste of the orient.

Place a layer of gravel in the base of the container to allow drainage of the pots and to provide humidity. While still in their pots, place your selection into your trough. As with other container plants, water and feed with a diluted liquid feed, and keep trimming as they are receiving light from one side only.

Remember to turn them regularly for even growth.

Hanging Baskets

A large flowerpot or pail is ideal to rest the basket on while planting. Line the basket with plastic sheeting and cut slits in the sides where you will be planting. Partially fill with a good proprietary hanging basket compost.

To insert the side plants through the liner it is wise to wrap them carefully in a sleeve of paper to protect roots and foliage from damage. Firm, and

continue to add compost and plant layers. Before inserting the top plants ensure you have a good lip of lining material for watering.

When planting is complete, give the basket a really good soaking and allow to drain. Place in a shady position until established and ready to hang out. Watering of the hanging basket is more intense as the nature of its position makes it susceptible to drying winds and hot sun all around. Watering twice a day in the summer is essential even if it rains, as the canopy of foliage will prevent rain permeating the soil. Regular feeding is also necessary due to the number of plants—diluted feed at every watering will do the trick. Regular picking and pruning will keep it tidy and bushy.

Creating a Herb Garden

The herb garden can be dated back to 2000BC in Egypt, where plants were grown for medicinal purposes. The later Roman gardens were geometric in style with a series of beds surrounded by low hedges. Each bed would contain herbs for different uses. In monasteries, herbs were needed in vast quantities to provide the monks with food and to provide medicines for the sick. Physic gardens were often found in English university towns to aid in the teaching of botany and medicine (many are now botanical gardens).

The Elizabethan English enjoyed the decorative and aromatic knot gardens while country folk grew their herbs as part of the whole garden, interspersing them with flowers, vegetables and fruit.

Any style of herb garden requires good preparation and planning to ensure it is a success.. Most herbs prefer a well-drained, medium (or even poor) soil, but all like their beds to be weed free. If possible, prepare the area the previous season, covering an area to cut out light as it's often the best way to clear a weedy patch. When the covering is removed then any remaining pernicious weeds can be dug out easily.

The Formal Garden

A formal garden will require a level surface. Design is important and is usually symmetrical, with each section surrounded by a low hedge. As you are going to live with the garden for a while do some research on the design you want. Formal designs are based on mathematics; the larger the area you have the better your design will look. The leveling of the site for a formal garden is worth the time and trouble. All you need are several measured pegs (marked at every 0.4 in. (1 cm) from the top), string, a straight-edged board, a mallet, and importantly, a spirit level. Choose your site carefully (remembering that most herbs enjoy the sunshine) and then mark it out with the pegs and string, making sure

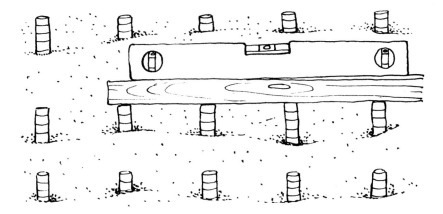

the prepared site is larger than the finished design. Set in your master peg at the highest level, to about 2 in. (5 cm) above the ground. Then systematically drive in pegs in a grid fashion, using the straight-edged board and spirit level, until they are all at the same level. The differences in soil level will be revealed by the marks on the sticks. You are then ready to add or remove soil to the same mark on each of the pegs, remembering to remove any weeds. This method should be adequate for a reasonably-sized plot and the next stage is to lay out the design.

In modern gardens space is often limited. However, a simple but effective design is a square with two diagonal paths meeting at a circle in the middle. This would give you four good-sized plots with a central feature.

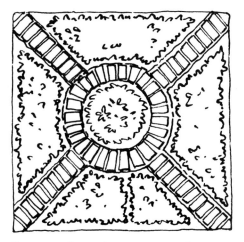

Once you have chosen your style, measure and peg it out in the garden.

Paths are the first thing to be laid. If you are choosing pavers then make sure they are laid well, with no weeds underneath. Cement them in place properly as opposed to laying them on a bed of sand; they are going to be there for a long time and need to be level and firm.

If your space is really limited then a cartwheel design dispensing with the hedging will give an equally good formal garden. The sections of the wheel are divided with paving, and the "hub" of the wheel provides the central feature. When planting, work from the center outward.

The central feature is the focal point, so should be considered carefully.

A columnar bay or rosemary kept well-clipped works well, but also this could be the place for an elegant birdbath, fountain, or even a tasteful statue.

For the hedgeless garden each section of the wheel can be graded in height from the tall central bay, with the next circle purple sage, on to marjoram and so on, down to thyme.

The hedged garden has each of the sections planted out. Sweet violets, lady's mantle, marjoram, calendula, chives, bergamot, feverfew, chamomile, or borage will give color and aroma while being useful in both the kitchen and the medicine chest. You may fill each section with one type of herb or, if the areas are larger, groups of herbs serving different purposes.

The final job is to plant the hedging; this is perhaps the most time consuming, as you will need a very large number of plants. Make sure you have sufficient numbers to complete the task, that

they are all bought from the same supplier, and are of the same age and size, to ensure regular even growth. Wall germander, hyssop, santolina, lavender, and box all make excellent low hedging plants. You may use the same species for the whole of the garden or you could try mirror hedges of different species. The combinations are endless, but the choice is yours and it gives you the opportunity to personalize your garden.

The Informal Garden

The informal garden is usually sited close to the house and consists of your favorite herbs readily available for you to pick for the cooking pot.

A popular option is the country-style mixed garden. Spread abundantly among flowers, fruit, and vegetables, the herbs combine to give a pleasing display while having the added value of attracting beneficial and beautiful wildlife into the garden.

An informal herb garden like this gives you a much wider scope and is more related to the herbaceous border, but careful planning is required to give the desired effect of "informality".

The use of rustic hazel archways, obelisks, or wigwams strategically placed will give added height.

Golden hops will scramble over these and entwine prettily with the brightly colored climbing nasturtiums.

To complement this try growing the taller angelica and lovage, along with soft feathery fennels rising majestically among the shrubby sage, rosemary, santolina, and curry plants.

Move down through to bergamot, sweet cicely and lemon balm to the marjorams, bright purple clumps of chives, and garlic chives. The bed edges will work well with low-growing thymes and patches of alpine strawberries tripping over the edge. A collection of annual flower seeds, such as cornflowers, love-in-the-mist (nigella), California poppies (eschscholzia) and calendula, strewn over the entire bed and left to its own devices, will always bring pleasant surprises and amazingly "tie" the bed together well.

The same principles apply whether planting an island bed or a border. Plan it carefully and use blocks of plants to create the informal look. Never plant less than three plants of a kind. Often five or even seven plants will make them look more "at home" in an informal garden.

Raised Beds

Should you have a heavy clay soil, often the easiest solution is to establish raised beds as the clay will not allow free draining. These can be made with all sorts of materials, from railway sleepers, bricks, and stone to decorative wattle sides.

Lay gravel in the bottom for better drainage, then fill with a suitable soil.

Plant taller herbs in the middle, working with smaller low-level herbs towards the edges. An interesting alternative is to grow different varieties of thyme in a raised bed and then use it as a living bench. The added advantage of raised beds is that less bending is needed to tend the gardens which makes them ideal for the less mobile gardener.

Planting

Selecting the right plants for your garden can be difficult, although the wonderful thing about herbs is their versatility, as many have culinary, medicinal, aromatic and natural dye uses.

Take into consideration the height and spread of each plant, the type of soil, sun or shade it likes, and the water it needs, and arrange accordingly. A visit to the nearest botanical garden or local herb nursery will give you a good idea of which plants work well together. Keep in mind the herbs that you actually use the most while planning.

Selecting a Good Plant

Always purchase plants from a good source, such as specialist nurseries, where they can offer advice concerning the plant growth and habit. Avoid plants sharing pots with weeds, and plants with sparse stems, discolored leaves, and limp or drooping sections. Check for pests and any signs of disease. Carefully upturn and take out of the pot to check that it is not root bound. Soil should be filling the pot and slightly moist, not shrinking from the sides and dry. Check the shape and vigor of the plant—any sign of "legginess" and the plant should be discarded.

How to Plant

Preparations should be completed over winter so that you can start planting in spring when the soil is warming up and moist. Place your plants in the positions you intend to plant them and make sure you are happy with the arrangement, remembering the eventual height and spread of each one.

Water the plants well before removing from the pots . With any that have become pot bound, gently tease out the roots to ensure a good start before planting. Watering during the first few weeks is essential to give the plants time to establish and acclimatize to their new surroundings.

Shade Lovers

There is a wealth of herbs that will
thrive in dappled shade, so no corner
of your garden need be left bare.
Shady areas could also be the place
to grow parsley. To avoid early bolting
with both parsley and ginger mint, cut
regularly to encourage new growth.

Lady's Mantle

French sorrel and the foamy flowers of lady's mantle will both thrive away from the glare of sunlight.

Mint

Many of the mint plants will run riot in damp shade so watch out and choose wisely. Ginger mint, with its green and gold leaves, will brighten the area.

Golden Feverfew

The pretty white daisy-like flowers of the golden feverfew will help to ease your migraine and brighten any dull corners of your garden.

Pulmonaria

Pulmonaria, with its spotted leaves and pretty pink and lilac-blue flowers, will also blossom in shady areas.

Sun Lovers

Most plants that have gray, fine foliage will enjoy full sun and thrive in it. The curry plant (*Helichrysum augustifolium*), will enjoy direct sunlight. While its yellow flowers can be dried for a spicy potpourri, it can alternatively be used for adding a mild curry flavor to dishes in cooking.

Marjoram

The marjoram's gold, green, and especially sweet form, with mounds of small aromatic leaves, is great sprinkled over pizzas and in stuffings.

Alecost

The taller alecost 12–52 in. (30–132 cm), or costmary, has spicy gray-green oval leaves and yellow button flowers late in the year. The leaves add a bite to salad.

Angelica

With a good moisture-retentive soil and plenty of well-mulched organic matter, the majestic angelica will thrive, growing to 5ft 9in. (1.8 m). It's a biennial, so for crystallizing use the young stems in the spring, and the leaves to sweeten fruit puddings.

Lovage

Lovage will live happily alongside majestic angelica, growing to 4ft 9in. (1.5 m) and can be used in herb breads as an alternative to garlic.

By the Pond

When developing a pond in the garden it is always wise to extend the liner to include a bog garden. One of the prettiest of herbs to grow by the water is meadowsweet. The clusters of tiny creamy-white flowers, smelling of almond, flower from June to August and are set off by finely-serrated dark green leaves. They can reach 24–48 in. (60–120 cm) and a group planted together appears as a sweet-smelling cloud. Its perfume lends itself to potpourris.

Purple loosestrife makes a pleasant partner to meadowsweet as its spikes of red-purple flowers growing slightly taller give an interesting contrast as they flower together.

Soapwort

We cannot forget soapwort, a handy herb that grows just where it is needed. The pretty pink clusters of flowers rise above the reddish-green stems with pale green leaves growing to 30 in. (76 cm). As its name suggests, this plant has been used down the ages as a cleanser.

Using the leaves, you will produce a fine green lather to clean your hands. However, when you boil the roots for a short while you can strain the liquid and use it as a shampoo, to wash the body, and for cleaning fine textiles. Apparently, the famous Bayeux tapestry was cleaned using this herb.

Chalk & Clay Survivors

While clay soils are often heavy and sticky they can be improved with the addition of horticultural grit and lots of organic matter.

Some deep-rooted plants, such as horseradish, are able to mine their way through clay soils. Make use of the plant by using only a small amount of root to make your own hot sauce, or use the leaves in a bath bag to ease aching joints.

Elecampane

One of the lesser-used but grander and more colorful herbs is elecampane, a sturdy plant growing to 60 in. (1.5 m). Rich, dark green leaves are complemented with large, bright yellow flowers, which are just like frayed sunflowers. After two years harvest the roots, clean them, and cut into sections to dry. After a while it will smell of violets.

Tansy

Tansy is a tough plant which will easily run rampant so keep a close eye on its spreading stolons (underground runners). It grows to 3 ft (1 m) with alternate feathery green leaves and flat clusters of yellow flowers between July and September. Cut several stems and hang in the kitchen to keep the flies away.

Steps 4,5 and 6

Step 7

Thyme

Thymus vulgaris, the culinary thyme, will fit well into nooks and crannies and can be used when rinsing hair to keep dandruff at bay. It is used in herbal remedies as a tonic and an antiseptic. Its leaves have, traditionally, been used for fabric dyeing.

Chives

Chives, part of the onion family, will also grow well in chalky soils. Use the chopped leaves in salads, or better yet, scatter the purple flowers over a green salad.

Maintenance

Maintenance is essential to the health
and vigor of the plants and for your
continued enjoyment of your garden.
Fortunately there is little to maintaining
a good herb garden for most herbs,
when in constant use, are being
continually trimmed. Keep the garden
weed free and the soil in good heart.
A light mulch will usually keep the
weeds down and keep the soil protected
from drying winds and sunshine.

A good pair of pruning shears is a vital tool in the herb garden. They should be used to remove diseased or dead parts of the plant.

Lavenders, santolinas, sages, artimesias and similar plants. all tend to become woody and leggy if left to their own devices. As a rule, cut back to a third and keep the plant's shape nicely rounded in late summer after flowering.

Low-growing thymes will tend to spread and leave a sparse center so trim back straggly growth in the fall. If the center is looking bare, sprinkle some potting mix to encourage rooting and new growth.

Plants with long-flowering stems like lovage, tansy, and fennel can have their stems cut right back to the ground. Formal gardens will also need hedge cutting in the growing season to keep them neat.

Lavender as a Border

Lavenders are aromatic, bush-forming plants useful for hedging and edging in borders. Coming in various heights and colors the two varieties most commonly used as edging plants because of their dwarf-growing habit are:

Lavandula augustifolia "Hidcote": height and spread 18–24 in. (45–60 cm) with deep purple-blue flowers.
Lavandula augustifolia "Nana alba": height and spread 6–15 in. (15–38 cm) with white flowers.

Plant lavenders for hedging at a distance of 9–12 in. (20–30 cm) apart. Pruning and clipping of lavenders is important as they can easily become straggly and leggy as they get older. Remove dead flower stems and trim plants in the fall, and cut back hard in late March–April to promote bushy growth from the base.

Lavender
Hardy evergreen shrubs with silver-gray, or gray-green, linear oblong leaves. Long spikes of flowers, ranging from white through pinks to purple. Height and spread from 6 in.–3 ft 9 in. (15 cm to 1.2 m) according to species. Plant September to March in well-drained soil in a sunny position.

Uses: aromatic, cosmetic, and medicinal.

Sage as Foliage

Sage plants are excellent in a sensory garden. Their leaves are soft and they have a delightful aroma. An entire bed of sages can be breathtaking as the different varieties come in a wide and vibrant array of colors. The gray-green of garden sage alongside the bright red or purple of purpurescens, or the stunning gold of icterina and the really fun variegated form, with its gray-green, cream-edged, pink-blushed leaves, will create a stunning addition to your garden.

During the summer these plants will be alive with the buzzing of bees, as sages all flower together and honey from sage is particularly tasty. Utilize the herbs by adding them to stuffings. If you have a sore throat in the winter they make excellent gargles.

Sage
A hardy evergreen and aromatic sub-shrub, height and spread 2–3 feet (60–90 cm).

The ovate, wrinkled leaves come in various colors, with flowers in white, pink, violet, or purple. Plant in ordinary, well-drained soil from September to March in a sunny position. Remove lower spikes after flowering and cut back hard in April to keep plants bushy and fresh.

Uses: culinary, medicinal, aromatic, tonic, and digestive.

Rosemary for Edging

The characteristic feature of the formal garden is sections of the design surrounded by low hedging. Box was most commonly used because of its dense foliage and slow growth. However, box is slow to propagate, taking two years to root, and another two before it is ready to plant out, which makes it expensive. A far easier, cheaper, and more fulfilling way to create hedging is to grow your own from seed, or from the cuttings of faster-maturing plants.

Rosemary

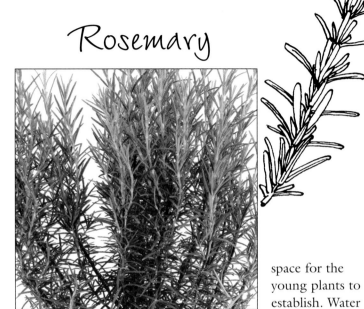

Rosemary is easy to propagate from half-ripe, 4 in. (10 cm) non-flowering shoots, taken in late July to August. These should be potted individually in a cold frame and will be ready for planting out the following May.

Make sure you have sufficient plants plus a few extra to complete the hedge. Clear the area for planting, allowing space for the young plants to establish. Water the pots and allow to drain. Plant at intervals of 15–20 in. (38–50 cm) to the same depth as they were in the pots. Water thoroughly and, as with all new transplants, ensure an adequate supply of water until established.

Keep the rosemary well trimmed to ensure growth is nice and bushy.

Thyme in Paving

Thymus Vulgaris and the golden form "Aureus" are the best culinary thymes. The wonderful fragrances and creeping low-growing habits of the myriad of other thymes make this plant ideal for use in those cracks and crevices found on the patio and pathways of our gardens. It is fun to make a perfumed path with collections of specific species as you move around the garden. Lemon-scented "citriodorus", caraway-scented "Corsican" and the pungent aroma of "ordinary" *thymus vulgaris* are but a few suggestions to get you started but a visit to a specialist nursery will offer a greater number of varieties to choose from.

Thyme

Thyme is a hardy perennial. A herbaceous sub-shrub, it varies from prostrate forms, to heights of 12 in. (30 cm). Leaves range in color from lemon-scented gold or variegated "silver posy", to various shades of gray-green through to green with flowers of white, through to pinks, reds, mauves, and purples.

Plant in any free-draining soil from October to March. Shear off flower heads after flowering to maintain dense growth.

Uses: for antibiotic, aromatic, medicinal, culinary purposes, and as a tonic to aid digestive problems.

Herbs in Gardening

All plants contain valuable nutrients and fiber, which are given up during the process of decay and may be returned to the soil to improve the structure and fertility. Several plants may be made into liquid fertilizers when broken down and diluted with water to form sprays. They are rich in specific nutrients and also have trace elements that enhance their use.

In an organic garden the herbs spread abundantly among the flowers and edible crops help to create a balance with nature. Herbs can be used to mask the scent of plants targeted by pests, or to encourage the predators. Many herbs in the past have been used as insecticides and fungicides when boiled up with a spot of soap added as a wetting agent. They also work as activators for compost heaps and as liquid fertilizers.

Hyssop

A hardy semi-evergreen perennial, with a bushy appearance that grows to 18 in. (45 cm). Aromatic, mid-green, narrow lance-shaped leaves in alternate opposite pairs and small purple-blue tubular flowers from July to September. Sow seeds in spring, grow on and plant in ordinary, well-drained soil in a sunny position in September. Remove flower stems after flowering. Hyssop is a good companion plant for all brassicas, helping to keep the cabbage white butterfly at bay, in combination with dill, which disguises the shape. It is useful when intermingled with crops but vulnerable to attack by sap-sucking aphids, as it works by inviting predators in to redress the balance.

Roman Chamomile

Perennial apple-scented creeping herb with mid-green leaves divided into fine leaflets giving a soft, feathery appearance. White daisy-like flowers with yellow centers on long stalks from May to September. Sow seeds in early spring, potted in small pots and plant out when the pots are filled with roots. Use as an edging around plants to attract hoverflies and lacewings to lay their eggs on vulnerable plants. The developing larvae will feed on aphids.

Garlic

Hardy perennial bulbous herb with segments or cloves. Hollow stems and clusters of pink-tinged white flowers in June to July. Plant individual cloves in well-drained, moisture-retentive fertile soil during October to February in a sunny position. To ensure good bulbs remove flower heads and harvest after foliage turns yellow.

Nettles

Nettles are a perennial herb with creeping yellow roots, hairy stems, and hairy, light green serrated leaves. Tiny green clusters of flowers blossom from June to September. Plant in direct sunlight, bordering the vegetable patch or close to the compost bin. Nettles gathered and placed in a container, covered with water and left for a couple of weeks to ferment, will render up a high nitrogen feed for your plants. When strained, dilute one part with ten parts of water, and use as a spray. Nettles are also an excellent activator in the compost bin when mixed with other material.

Russian Comfrey

Another hardy perennial with hairy branched stems that grow up to 3 ft 9 in. (1.2 m) in length with large, long, dark green, hairy leaves. Bell-shaped blue-purple flowers hang in clusters during May to October. Plant rooted offsets in well-manured soil in April to September, keep weeded and watered in the first year and mulch annually with compost. Comfrey will usefully "mine" valuable potassium, along with other trace elements, with its long taproot.

Cut comfrey (it can be cut several times during the growing season) before it flowers to maintain the high levels of nutrients in the leaves and stems. The wilted leaves (always let

them wilt before use on the soil or they may root and grow) are useful when placed in potato trenches to help prevent scab on the tubers. They can also be used as a mulch around potassium-loving plants, and they will retain moisture. As they decay they enrich the potassium levels in the soil, making them useful around fruit and flowering plants.

An excellent high-potassium liquid feed may be made by setting a container, with a hole drilled into the base, on bricks. Place a receptacle beneath the hole and fill the container with comfrey, pressing it firmly down. Cover and leave to ferment for a few weeks. The resulting viscous black liquid can be diluted (one part to fifteen) with water. Excellent for container-grown tomatoes, flowers, beans and so on.

Harvesting
& Preserving

There are many ways of preserving the flavor of herbs: drying, freezing, crystallizing, or putting in oil or vinegars. However you choose to preserve them they need to be harvested while at their very best. Early in the season, just before flowering, volatile oils contained in the leaves will be at their maximum. Picking early in the day just after the dew has evaporated is the optimum time and will give the best results. Material for harvesting should be clean, free of any blemishes, and with no pests evident. Be gentle when harvesting and use sharp pruners. Gently lay the cut herbs out in a flat trug, basket, or box and have a cloth over the handle or across the box (not lying on the herbs), to shade them until you can get them into the kitchen.

Drying

Always handle the herbs with care as any bruising will detract from the quality of the dried herb. Tie the sprigs of herbs in bunches and hang in a warm, dark atmosphere with good ventilation and check regularly. A warm cupboard is a suitable place. Once the herbs are dried they should feel brittle to the touch and rustle when moved.

To keep dried herbs strip the leaves from the stems and store in dark-colored glass or ceramic containers with well-fitting lids.
Store away from direct sunlight.

Dry seeds by tying paper bags around the bunches of seed heads and hanging in a well-ventilated, warm place to dry. Shake out dried seeds from seed heads and pick out the debris before storing in paper bags in jars.

Freezing

The freshly harvested, clean herbs are easy to freeze. Place in quick-sealed bags and pop in the freezer. When frozen, quickly divide into small portions, re-seal and keep in a container. Alternatively, chop the herbs quickly and pop into ice cube trays, cover with water and fast-freeze for adding to soups and casseroles. The frozen cubes can be stored in polythene bags ready for use.

Oils & Vinegars

Herb flavors can be preserved by steeping them in oil or vinegars. Simply add herbs to the oils or vinegars for a week, changing the herbs for fresh ones at least three times during the period, until the flavor is strong enough. Finish off the bottles by placing a sprig of the herb in the bottle before sealing.

Crystallizing

Crystallizing is the ideal way to preserve flowers for decoration; try primroses, violets, or rose petals.

First, carefully wash and dry a cupful of flowers. Boil a cupful of water with 8 oz (510 g) of sugar until the temperature reaches 239 °F (115 °C). Drop in a dozen flowers, leave for no more than a minute and then remove the syrup-coated flowers to a tin foil-covered tray. Once all are coated, place the tray into a warm oven to dry, turning once. Store in airtight tins layered between wax paper. You can also dip the petals in egg white and then coat these in confectioner's sugar. This method isn't appropriate for keeping flowers for any length of time but is suitable for use the same day.

Dyeing

The earliest written record of the use of dyestuffs is in China. Leaves, flowers, bark, berries, and roots of various herbs are all used in natural dyeing. Stains from berries and plants have been used as colorants in cave paintings, and for coloring foods and fabrics.

They have also been used to "paint" faces and bodies in order for them to be both admired and feared; Queen Boudicca in AD 60 anointed her body with woad before riding into battle against the Romans at Colchester, England.

The three main fabric herb dyes in 1290 were woad (blue), madder (browny-pinks and oranges), and weld (yellows and golds). Today there are many garden plants which are excellent dye plants that will provide a rainbow of colors, although they may not be colorfast unless the fabric is first treated with a mordant.

Mordants

Mordants are used to "fix" color. In the past, natural mordants such as rock alum, tea leaves or club mosses, stale urine, wood ash and rhubarb leaves were used, depending on which colors were needed.

Sorrel

Pot Marigold

Hardy perennial reaching up to 40 in. (100 cm). Fleshy mid-green arrow-shaped, sharp lemon-flavored leaves, red-green flower spikes in June and July. Plant or divide established plants in spring or fall in well-drained fertile soil, in sun or partial shade. Plants should be replaced after three to four years. The tops of sorrel will give pink colors with a mordant of vinegar or dark olive colors with a mordant of ammonia.

Annual branched, stemmed plant, with pale green, long oval leaves, large daisy-like orange flowers from May to first frosts. Sow seeds in well-drained medium garden soil in situ, covering with 0.4 in. (1 cm) of soil in spring for summer flowering, and in the fall for spring flowering. Contains calendulin, a yellow coloring substance, used to color cheese and butter. Petals can be used as a substitute for expensive saffron when coloring rice dishes.

Aromatic Herbs

The potency of aromatic herbs has been used in various ways over the centuries. Herbs have, in the past, been strewn on floors, in front of processions, and also used in the form of potpourri that we know today.

Around the home, herbs have been used for herbal sachets, for pomanders in the linen cupboard, for relaxing herbal baths, and also made into oils for massage. The medicinal qualities of aromatic herbs certainly haven't gone unnoticed, and have been used to ward off disease, as disinfectants and deodorizers, to make toilet waters, and burned to cleanse sick rooms.

In ancient Egypt scented oils were used for massage, while the Romans scented their famous baths with herbs.

Apothecary's Rose

Deciduous thorny-stemmed shrub with height and spread of 35 in. (90 cm). Leaves consist of three or five dark green leaflets. Light crimson flowers during May to June followed by large, round red hips. Plant in well-drained moisture-retentive soil in a sunny position between October and April. Mulch well.

Aromatic uses:
Rose water is used in perfumes, toilet waters, cosmetics and talcum powders. Sprinkle rose water onto a flannel and add to the dryer for sweetly-scented bed linen. Rose petals can be dried and used in potpourri, or made into scented beads or massage oils.

Aromatic uses:
Strewing herb. Dried flowers and leaves can be used to repel moths and insects. When made into sachets it can be placed among the linen or can be rubbed on insect bites to relieve pain.

Cotton Lavender

Hardy evergreen dwarf shrub. Silvery-gray, finely dissected aromatic leaves form 18–24 in. (45–60 cm) mound with bright yellow flowers in July.

Plant in the fall or spring in ordinary, well-drained soil in full sunshine. Prune hard back after flowering or in spring to keep from becoming leggy.

Index of
Herbs

NAME:	Alecost (Balsamita major)
APPEARANCE:	Slender serrated leaves, yellow button flowers
PROPAGATION:	Divide roots in spring or fall, dry sunny position
USES:	Aromatic, astringent, and antiseptic

NAME:	Angelica (Archangelica officinalis)
APPEARANCE:	Tall (5ft 10 in/1.8 m) green sectioned leaves, pale greenish-yellow flower clusters
PROPAGATION:	Divide roots or seed, plant in shaded good soil
USES:	Crystallized stems, sweetener in fruit, and assists digestion

NAME:	Apothecary's Rose (Rosa Gallica Officinalis)
APPEARANCE:	Thorny stems, strongly perfumed, light crimson flowers, large red hips
PROPAGATION:	Plant in deep rich soil in a sunny position
USES:	Aromatic, potpourri, rose water, jams, and vinegars

NAME:	Basil Sweet (Ocimum basilicum)
APPEARANCE:	Bright green, oval leaves, small creamy flowers
PROPAGATION:	Annual grown from seed from May onward, prone to frost damage
USES:	Salads, pesto sauce, digestive, and as snuff

NAME:	Bay (Laurus Nobilis)
APPEARANCE:	Glossy leather-like lance-shaped leaves, small yellow-green flowers in spring
PROPAGATION:	Plant in spring, in ordinary soil, in sunny sheltered position
USES:	Aromatic, potpourri, bouquets garnis, soups, and stews

NAME:	Bergamot (Monarda didyma)
APPEARANCE:	Dark green leaves, bright red flowers
PROPAGATION:	Rich moist soil Oct, March, April, sun or partial shade, mulch well
USES:	Leaves for salads, flowers and leaves for potpourri. Oswego tea

NAME:	Borage (Borago officinalis)
APPEARANCE:	Hairy stalks and leaves, star-like flowers
PROPAGATION:	Sow seeds in spring, suitable for most soils, likes chalk
USES:	Anti-inflammatory, great in summer drinks and salads
NAME:	Chamomile (Chamaemelum nobile)
APPEARANCE:	Branched hairy stems with feathery leaves. White daisy-like flowers, yellow centers
PROPAGATION:	Sow seeds in spring in rich loamy soil
USES:	Digestive, antibiotic, spray "for damping off", potpourri, and calming tea
NAME:	Chervil (Anthriscus cerefolium)
APPEARANCE:	Pale green, lacy leaves and white flowers
PROPAGATION:	Sow in spring at regular intervals for continuous use
USES:	Soups, salads, and digestive tea
NAME:	Chives (Allium schoenoprasum)
APPEARANCE:	Long thin green leaves from bulb, purple pom-pom flowers
PROPAGATION:	Plant in good fertile soil in sun or partial shade
USES:	Flowers and leaves in salads
NAME:	Comfrey (Russian comfrey – Symphytum x uplandicum)
APPEARANCE:	Long, dark green, hairy leaves. Bell-shaped blue-purple flowers
PROPAGATION:	Root division in fall to spring. Mulch well and cut often
USES:	Fertilizer, compost activator, ointments for bruising, healing, and softening
NAME:	Coriander (Coriandrum sativum)
APPEARANCE:	Lower leaves broad-scalloped, upper leaves feathery, mauve-colored flowers
PROPAGATION:	Sow in early spring, light soil in sun, harvest seeds in August
USES:	Leaves in salads, stews; seeds in curries and other spicy dishes, potpourri

NAME:	Cotton lavender (Santolina chamaecyparissus)
APPEARANCE:	Finely divided, aromatic, gray leaves and yellow button flowers
PROPAGATION:	Plant in the fall in well-drained soil in full sun, set plants at least 2 feet (30 cm) apart.
USES:	Aromatic, potpourri, and insect repellent

NAME:	Cowslips (Primula veris)
APPEARANCE:	Green rosette of leaves, clusters of yellow flowers on erect 4–12 in. (10–30 cm) stems
PROPAGATION:	Sow seeds in spring in shady, damp position
USES:	Wine, tea, and leaves in salads

NAME:	Curry plant (Helichrysum augustifolium)
APPEARANCE:	Aromatic gray needle-like leaves, yellow flower clusters
PROPAGATION:	Plant in ordinary, well-drained soil in a sunny position
USES:	Aromatic, potpourri, mild curry flavor in soups, rice etc.

NAME:	Dill (Anthum graveolens)
APPEARANCE:	Tall, dark-striped stems with feathery leaves, clusters of yellow flowers
PROPAGATION:	Sow seeds at regular intervals from April to June
USES:	Leaves in salads, good with fish, pickles and seeds improve cabbage water

NAME:	Elecampane (Inula helenium)
APPEARANCE:	Tall-growing, large green leaves with bright yellow flowers
PROPAGATION:	Grow in ordinary, rich soil in a moist sunny position
USES:	Roots candied, cook as a vegetable, dried in potpourri

NAME:	Fennel (Foeniculum vulgare)
APPEARANCE:	Tall-growing, feathery-leaved, clusters of yellow flowers
PROPAGATION:	Sow seeds in spring or divide roots in March
USES:	Leaves in salads, seeds with fish, in bread, in cooking cabbage. Dye plant

NAME:	Feverfew (Tanaceteum parthenium)
APPEARANCE:	Yellow-green divided leaves, white daisy-like flowers with yellow centers
PROPAGATION:	Sow seeds in spring in well-drained soil in a sunny position
USES:	A sandwich of leaves will help alleviate a migraine
NAME:	Garlic (Allium sativum)
APPEARANCE:	Bulb of several cloves, flat thin leaves. White starry clusters of flowers
PROPAGATION:	Individual cloves planted in spring in most soils in sun
USES:	Antiseptic, antibiotic, diuretic, expectorant. Cloves as flavoring, insect repellent
NAME:	Great Mullein (Verbascum thapsus)
APPEARANCE:	Soft hairy stems and gray-green leaves. Spike of yellow flowers
PROPAGATION:	Sow in spring in sunny sheltered site in poor soil. Self-sows
USES:	Fresh flowers made into an ointment for wounds and piles
NAME:	Hops (Humulus lupulus)
APPEARANCE:	Climbing heart-shaped green leaves, yellow-green cone-like flowers
PROPAGATION:	Plant out in rich, moist soil in a sunny position
USES:	Raw shoots in salads. Flowers in hop pillows or brewed as a tea for insomnia
NAME:	Horseradish (Armoracia rusticana)
APPEARANCE:	Deep-rooting, large green leaves, white aromatic flowers
PROPAGATION:	Plant in rich moist soil in spring in a sunny position
USES:	Aids digestion, antibiotic, and root used for sauce
NAME:	Hyssop (Hyssopus officinalis)
APPEARANCE:	Evergreen plant, small green leaves, light blue to purple flowers
PROPAGATION:	Plant in light soil in a sunny position
USES:	Hyssop tea for rheumatism. Lotion relieves insect stings

NAME:	Lady's Mantle (Alchemilla vulgaris)
APPEARANCE:	Kidney-shaped green leaves, foamy green flowers
PROPAGATION:	Plant in moisture-retentive soil in partial shade, October to March
USES:	Astringent, tea for period pains
NAME:	Lavender (Lavandula augustifolia)
APPEARANCE:	Long narrow gray-green leaves, violet-colored spikes of flowers
PROPAGATION:	Well-drained soil in sunny position, cut back regularly
USES:	Digestive, culinary, potpourri, relaxing tea and oil
NAME:	Lemon balm (Melissa officinalis)
APPEARANCE:	Pale green nettle-like and lemon-scented leaves, small white tubular flowers
PROPAGATION:	Plant in October to March in well-drained soil in sun or semi-shade
USES:	Potpourri, relaxing tisane, bath herb. Flavoring, salads
NAME:	Lemon Grass (Cymbopogon citratus)
APPEARANCE:	Aromatic grass, long, thin green leaves, clusters of green flowers tinged with red
PROPAGATION:	Plant indoors in direct sunlight
USES:	Aromatic oil used in perfumes. Leaves used in Thai cuisine
NAME:	Lovage (Levisticum officinale)
APPEARANCE:	Large dark green leaves, clusters of small yellow flowers
PROPAGATION:	Plant in the fall in rich and well-drained soil in sun or partial shade
USES:	Culinary, celery-like flavor in salads, herb breads. Diuretic
NAME:	Lungwort (Pulmonaria officinalis)
APPEARANCE:	Basal leaves, oval, hairy with pale green blotches. Pink to lilac bell flowers
PROPAGATION:	Plant October to March in ordinary moist soil in the shade
USES:	Beneficial for coughs and colds

NAME:	Marjoram (Origanum vulgare)
APPEARANCE:	Aromatic dark green leaves, small clusters of lilac flowers on long branching stems
PROPAGATION:	Plant in the sun in spring; cut back before tying down to a third in winter
USES:	Used in bouquet garni, sedative, antiseptic, potpourri, herb pillows, a rub for rheumatism

NAME:	Meadowsweet (Filipendula ulmanaria)
APPEARANCE:	Serrated dark green leaves, clusters of creamy white flowers smelling of almond
PROPAGATION:	Plant October–March in moist, fertile alkaline soil in sun or partial shade
USES:	Flowers dried in potpourri and sachets for bed linen

NAME:	Mint (Mentha)
APPEARANCE:	Creeping plant with various shades of oval- to lance-shaped leaves
PROPAGATION:	Plant in moist well-drained soil during spring or fall
USES:	Culinary and antiseptic uses. Scattered leaves can deter mice and rats

NAME:	Nasturtiums (Trapaeolum Majus)
APPEARANCE:	Umbrella-like green leaves, bright red, orange and yellow flowers
PROPAGATION:	Annual plant, sow seeds during spring in situ
USES:	Leaves and flowers in salads, green seeds may be pickled as caper substitutes

NAME:	Catmint (Nepeta cataria)
APPEARANCE:	Gray-green aromatic nettle-like leaves, pink flowers
PROPAGATION:	Divide or sow plants in spring in well-drained soil in sun or dappled shade
USES:	Young leaves in salad. Digestive, sedative, and insecticide

NAME:	Nettles (Urtica dioica)
APPEARANCE:	Yellow roots, hairy stems, and serrated leaves. Clustered tiny green flowers
PROPAGATION:	Plant in direct sunlight; suitable for most soil types
USES:	Tea, insecticide, compost activator, hair rinse, and dye plant

NAME:	Parsley (Petroselinum crispum)
APPEARANCE:	Shiny green-lobed, flat or curly leaves, yellow flowers in dense clusters
PROPAGATION:	Sow in situ February to June in well-drained, fertile soil in sun or partial shade
USES:	Bouquet garni, in fish dishes, in salads, and as a breath freshener
NAME:	Pot marigold (Calendula officinalis)
APPEARANCE:	Pale green oval leaves and orange flowers
PROPAGATION:	Sow seeds in any soil during spring in a sunny position
USES:	Dye plant, potpourri, as a soothing ointment and flowers, good in salads
NAME:	Primrose (Primula vulgaris)
APPEARANCE:	Rosette of wrinkled green leaves with sweet-smelling pale yellow flowers
PROPAGATION:	Plant during October to March in fertile soil, in sun or partial shade
USES:	Potpourri, salads, and as a herbal tea
NAME:	Purple loosestrife (Lythrum salicaria)
APPEARANCE:	Spikes of purple flowers rise above stems with long green leaves
PROPAGATION:	Plant in ordinary moist garden soil, in sun or semi-shade
USES:	Decoction used in the treatment of diarrhea
NAME:	Rosemary (Rosmarinus officinalis)
APPEARANCE:	Green needle-like leaves, mauve flowers
PROPAGATION:	Plant in ordinary, well-drained garden soil in a sunny position
USES:	Digestive, stimulates circulation, good with lamb, jellies, and in potpourri
NAME:	Sage (Salvia officinalis)
APPEARANCE:	Gray-green oblong leaves with white woolly undersides, violet flowers
PROPAGATION:	Plant March to April in well-drained light soil in a sunny position
USES:	Stuffings, flavoring for meat dishes. Astringent and tea. Gargle for sore throats

Index of Herbs

NAME:	*Soapwort (Saponaria officinalis)*
APPEARANCE:	*Pale green leaves, pink clusters of flowers*
PROPAGATION:	*Plant Oct–Mar in sun or partial shade. Cut to ground level in the fall*
USES:	*Cleansing properties for fabrics, skin, and hair*
NAME:	*Sorrel (Rumex acidosa)*
APPEARANCE:	*Fleshy mid-green arrow-shaped, lemon-flavored leaves, red-green flower spikes*
PROPAGATION:	*Divide established plants in spring or fall in well-drained fertile soil in sun*
USES:	*Dye plant, diuretic, laxative, astringent. Leaves in salads and sauces*
NAME:	*St John's Wort (Hypericum perfuratum)*
APPEARANCE:	*Oval leaves with translucent dots, small golden yellow clusters of flowers*
PROPAGATION:	*Plant in October and April in fertile, well-drained soil in the sun*
USES:	*Oil useful for rheumatism rub, softens skin, tea for lightening depression*
NAME:	*Sweet Cicely (Myrrhis odorata)*
APPEARANCE:	*Large downy, feathery light green leaves, white compound clusters of flowers*
PROPAGATION:	*Sow seeds in March or April in a weed-free bed*
USES:	*Leaves as sugar substitute in baking, boiled root used in salads*
NAME:	*Tansy (Tanacetum vulgare)*
APPEARANCE:	*Finely divided feathery leaves, yellow clusters of button flowers*
PROPAGATION:	*Plant during fall or spring. Creeping roots spread rapidly*
USES:	*Insecticide and everlasting flower when dried*
NAME:	*Thyme (Thymus vulgaris most common variety)*
APPEARANCE:	*Low-growing small leaves, various colored flowers from white through to purple*
PROPAGATION:	*Plant in spring and fall in light, well-drained soil in direct sunlight*
USES:	*Culinary, bouquet garni, potpourri, digestive, and antiseptic*